STEPPING

UP

**10 Take-Aways
for Advancing Your Career**

Simple Truths is a registered trademark.
Printed and bound in the United States of America.
ISBN 978-1-60810-195-5
www.simpletruths.com
Toll Free 800-900-3427
Book Design: Brian Frantz

WOZ 10 9 8 7 6 5 4 3 2

Table of Contents: Stepping Up

THE 10 TAKE-AWAYS

Foreword

By Mac Anderson

I got the call about a year ago. It was from author John Murphy, who said, "Mac, I've got a good idea for a book."

Well, here's the deal. When John has an idea, I've learned…it's almost always good.

In the last 25 years, I've had the privilege of meeting and working with many authors. Some, in fact, have been #1 on the *New York Times* best-seller list. However, John Murphy has developed the art of saying "more" with "less" than any author I've ever known. So many times I've said, "It's not **what** you say, but **how** you say it that turns the switch from 'off' to 'on.' John's writing style is clear, concise and engaging. He asks questions to make you think and makes his point in a way that makes the reader say, "Wow. I never thought of it quite that way!"

John has written three best-sellers for Simple Truths:

- **Pulling Together**…*10 Rules for High Performance Teamwork*
- **Leading with Passion**…*10 Essentials for Inspiring Others*
- **The How of Wow**…*Secrets to World Class Service*

He and I also collaborated on another book that has struck a chord with our readers… **Habits Die Hard**.

I'm now honored to publish his latest book, **Stepping Up**…*10 Takeaways for Advancing Your Career*. If you're totally pleased with the success you've had in your career and in life, you can stop reading now. If, however, you'd like to "step up" and tap into your true potential, this book is for you.

I challenge you to read and re-read John's advice for making your career and your life all it can be. His engaging book will show you how to respond to the abundance that is all around us.

And one more thing, share it with a friend or co-worker. They might just be ready to "step up!"

In *Stepping Up* and its ten take-away lessons, John has packaged everything you need to accelerate success in your career…in your life. As John would say, it's time to *Step Up or Step Aside!*

All the Best,

Mac Anderson
Founder, Simple Truths

INTRODUCTION

"I know of no more encouraging fact than
the unquestionable ability of man to elevate
his life by conscious endeavor."
~ Henry David Thoreau

Listen carefully to successful people all over the world and they will tell you one thing. **Opportunity quietly surrounds you.** Information and knowledge are within your reach. Prosperity is silently knocking at your door. Victory mysteriously awaits you. Subtle and elusive as it may seem, there is no scarcity of success. It is available to all of us. The only real problem is how we choose to respond to the unlimited abundance that is ours for the taking.

Do we accept it or reject it?

Do we allow it or resist it?

Do we demand it or dismiss it?

Do we take it in or turn it away?

Stop and ask yourself:

How do you see the world?

How do you see yourself in the world?

How do you see your relationship with the world?

Do you see the opportunity?

Do you believe it is yours for the taking?

Do you feel worthy of success?

Do you feel deserving?

Are you asking for it?

Are you looking for it?

Are you listening for it?

Are you open to it?

Are you allowing it to manifest in your life and your presence, or have you convinced yourself that you do not qualify for one reason or another?

Are you seizing the opportunity to advance yourself and the world in a mutually beneficial way or are you putting it off for another day?

Are you expecting success or suspecting it?

Are you even aware the choice is up to you?

I am fortunate to work with many successful executives, professionals, military leaders, authors, consultants, teachers, parents, coaches and athletes around the world, and a term I hear more and more frequently is "Step Up." From North America to China to Brazil to countries all over Europe, the mantra is the same. *We need people to step up*. We believe in them. We see the potential. We know they can do better. We want them to succeed. We just need to see them take charge and step up.

In other cases, proactive people are advancing themselves without being asked or encouraged. They just do it, often surprising the people around them. They use the ten "take-aways" described in this book to tap into their true potential. This illustrates that we do not need permission to step up. We do not need to be told to do it, or even asked. We can apply these take-aways to our personal and professional lives wherever and whenever we want.

The key is to know that we can step up and then to know how!

The purpose of this book is to explain
how to step up and accelerate success.

Why wait?
Why not seize the moment?
Why not get started immediately?
Why make excuses that limit us?
Why rationalize our undesirable results
and restrict ourselves?

This book is not about self-imposed resistance to change. It is about flow. It is about energy. It is about movement and motivation, insight and inspiration. It is about "taking away" lessons learned from the best of the best, people who in many cases overcame tremendous odds to reach levels of performance and prosperity that many only dream of. Take these tips and use them to elevate your life.

Use this book and these take-aways to:

- [ ] Take ownership and responsibility for your outcomes

- [ ] Take a good, honest look in the mirror

- [ ] Take time to reflect on who you are and what you are capable of

- [ ] Take measure of your current state—the good, the bad and the ugly!

- [ ] Take advice from wise counsel

- [ ] Take a chance

- [ ] Take action

- [ ] Take another look at your life and your results

- [ ] Take a knee and give thanks for what you are and what you have

#1

TAKE OWNERSHIP

"Two roads diverged in a wood, and
I–I took the one less traveled by, and
that has made all the difference."

~ Robert Frost

Peak performance requires mental, physical and emotional ownership. Mind, body and soul must be focused, aligned and passionate about stepping up and delivering results. There is no room in this equation for procrastination, doubt, excuses, blame, denial or resistance.

TAKE-AWAY #1 TRANSLATES INTO:

Take charge.
Raise your hand.
Volunteer.
Visualize success.
Focus.
Make a commitment.
Be responsible.
Set an example.
Make something happen.
Connect the dots.
See it through.
Get it done.
Be accountable.

Many of my clients struggle with taking ownership. Organizationally, culturally and individually, there is often a tendency to shift responsibility, deny accountability, rationalize waste and point the finger. I see it all the time. It exists in business, government, education and health care. It is as if the senior leadership is inviting people to take a risk and step up, but relatively few proactively accept the call, including many people already in positions of management and leadership! It seems they would rather play it safe, standing on the sidelines instead of getting into the game.

What is holding them back? Is it fear, insecurity, doubt or disbelief? Is it ignorance, pride or ego?

These are questions every leader must contemplate because without a true sense of ownership, the organization is paralyzed. Fear and blame are disempowering energies. Ignorance and ego are limiting factors. We need ownership to overcome these self-imposed constraints. Successful people know this and do something about it.

When I was in high school, I experienced a devastating accident. I was working on a lawn crew and I cut my foot severely with a lawn mower. Six days in the hospital and ten hours of surgery later, I was told by an award-winning, internationally-renowned surgeon that I would never play football again—a passion of mine at the time—and that I would be lucky to walk again without limping. I wept with grief and remorse. At age 17, what was I to do now?

The year was 1977 and in those days lawn mowers did not have many of the safety features they have today. Perhaps I could argue that it was the lawn mower manufacturer's fault? In a very litigious society, there are certainly many who might agree. Maybe it was the homeowner's fault? After all, she asked me to cut down a stretch of tall field grass along the side of her house. This was not part of our original deal and the tall grass was full of rocks, one of which I tripped over. Maybe I could blame the rock? Or maybe I could blame the surgeon or the work schedule or my shoes or the stars?

Truth be told, I owned it. It was my foot, my doing, my life. It was my choice to play victim or champion. I stood at a mystical fork in the road called life and I had to decide which way to go. I chose ownership. I opted to take charge and be responsible for moving forward in a positive way, not wallowing in grief over something I could not undo.

This road made all the difference.

Three years later, I was playing football for the University of Notre Dame, tapping a sign on Saturdays that reads, "Play like a champion today."

"The instinct of ownership
is fundamental in man's nature"

~ William James

CHECKLIST FOR SUCCESS:

- [ ] I take charge.

- [ ] I visualize success and see myself accomplishing great things.

- [ ] I make a commitment and keep my word.

- [ ] I am part of the solution, not the problem.

- [ ] I find ways to connect the dots and pull people together.

- [ ] I see things through and get things done.

#2

TAKE NOTES

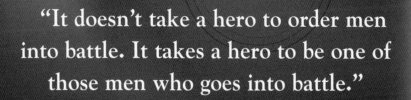

"It doesn't take a hero to order men into battle. It takes a hero to be one of those men who goes into battle."

~ General H. Norman Schwarzkopf

I am always intrigued with how resistant some people are to new ideas, new insights, new information and new discoveries.

Why go through life with the brakes on?

Why attempt to move forward by looking through a rear-view mirror?

Why resist growth?

Why put energy into protecting flawed assumptions of the past when new evidence reveals they are no longer valid?

Why not listen to progress and take notes from people who are masterful at that which we desire?

Socrates once said, "We have two ears and one mouth. We should use them proportionately." I love this comment because it reveals a very empowering and simple truth. We are wise to listen. We are wise to ask questions. We are wise to seek understanding.

When we approach life with an open and curious mind, we learn at a much faster pace. Life then shows itself as the true adventure that it is. It is a journey of creation, exploration and uncertainty. It is an experience of experimentation, growth and learning. It is an opportunity to prosper and help others prosper. It is a time to generate and be generous.

Taking notes means paying attention with an open, non-judgmental mind. It means temporarily suspending analysis, criticism and disbelief while seeking true understanding and awareness.

I took note when I rested in the hospital recovering from my foot injury. My grandfather sent me a book titled, *On Courage*. One of the featured stories in the book was about Rocky Bleier, a four-time Super Bowl winner who overcame very serious injuries from the war in Vietnam. As it turned out, Rocky put "mind over matter" and did what the doctors said he could not do. He returned to playing football and went on to be a starting running back for the Pittsburgh Steelers. Make no mistake, these were notes I paid very close attention to.

☐ What notes are you taking in life and where are you getting them?

☐ Are you asking the right questions of the right people?

☐ Are you doing your homework?

☐ Are you keeping an open mind?

☐ Are you preparing yourself for the next step up?

☐ Are you tapping into the abundant resources all around you for ideas and insights on how to improve your life?

☐ What new tools, techniques or practices have you identified that will accelerate your success?

☐ What are you doing with these tools?

We are all creatures of habit. **Take note** of your habits and examine your tendencies carefully. **Pay attention** to the habits of others as well, especially the people who are demonstrating the behavior and results you seek. **Interview** them if you get the chance. **Read** their stories. **Listen** to their secrets. **Embrace** their examples. I will never forget the day I was scheduled to work with General H. Norman Schwarzkopf, the military leader in charge of Desert Storm. To prepare for the meeting and the day I would spend traveling with him, I read his entire 530-page autobiography. It made for a very meaningful conversation on leadership and a few important "take aways" I will never forget. I now keep this autographed book on the same shelf as the book *On Courage*, subsequently signed by Rocky.

What a difference a few good books
and role models can make!

CHECKLIST FOR SUCCESS:

☐ I listen with an open mind.

☐ I see all interactions with people as an opportunity to learn.

☐ I pay attention to the attitudes and behaviors of successful people.

☐ I seek advice from wise people.

☐ I do not take constructive criticism personally.

☐ I invite "push back" and alternative points of view.

#3

TAKE A GOOD, HONEST LOOK IN THE MIRROR

"Whether you think you can or you think you can't, you're right."

~ Henry Ford

What does the universe reflect back at you?
Stop and think about it.
What are you reaping?

Now ask yourself:
What are you sowing?
Do you see the correlation?
Are you looking for it?
Do you understand the law of cause and effect?
Make no mistake, there is a relationship.
It is universal law. **What we give is what we get!**

People with "abundance-consciousness" realize that the more we give, the more we have to give. The more we help others, the more others help us. The more we contribute, the more we have to contribute. The more we give love, the more love we have to give. It is a paradox. The more we give joy, the more joy we feel. The more we forgive, the more we are forgiven. We are essentially limitless "channels" of energy. There is no shortage of the things that matter most. Scarcity is an illusion. Flow is abundant. The amount of success I achieve does not take away from anyone else's success.

People with "victim-consciousness" or "poverty-consciousness" do not see or accept this correlation. They do not understand the paradox. They do not make the connection between inputs and outputs, or cause and effect. As a result, they suffer without any sense of responsibility, ownership and accountability. They see the world as scarce and go through life with the brakes on. As a result of this perception, they are simply receiving what they are putting forth—which is often very little or very negative. If I have doubt, for example, the world will deliver back to me all the evidence I need to remain doubtful. Thus, it will always appear to be someone else's fault or responsibility. There will never be enough time. There will seem to be no alternatives, but plenty of excuses. Things will never change unless my consciousness changes. I will continue to assume it is up to someone else to solve my problems, which will not happen. A shift in awareness is the only way to break these habits and step up.

A mirror can tell us a lot. For example, it allows us to see the lines on our faces as we age.

What do these lines reveal over time?
A perpetual scowl?
A habitual frown?
A natural smile?
A look of stress, anger, sadness or joy?
Is there hope written on your face?
Or gratitude?
Is there a positive twinkle in your eyes
or a look of fear and hesitation?

Pay attention to your body language.

How do you stand or sit or move about?
What does your posture say to people?

Stepping up requires that we take note of our own brutal facts— the good, the bad and the ugly.

☐ What are we blessed with?

☐ What competencies and skills do we have to offer the world?

☐ What hindrances and challenges do we need to overcome?

☐ What help do we need?

☐ What help can we offer?

☐ How can we best leverage our strengths and offset our limitations?

☐ More than anything, what is our "altitude" telling us about our attitude?

☐ What do we truly believe about what we can and can't do?

☐ Why do we think this way?

☐ What mental and emotional programs are governing our lives, consciously and subconsciously?

Use the mirror as a metaphor for carefully examining the relationship between what we sow and what we reap. There can be no positive change in outputs without a positive change in inputs. Find the right levers and you can move the world.

When I gave my first public seminar in 1988, I invited a trusted university professional to attend the event and give me feedback. My intentions were positive and my interest was in learning ways to improve my performance. I wanted to step up. The written evaluations for the seminar were very positive and I secured two new clients as a result. I had every reason to believe I did a great job. Still, I asked for candid feedback. I knew I could do better. To this day, my colleague's words echo in my mind. She simply asked me if I wanted the truth. Right there, I knew she had some constructive criticism to offer. This might hurt. Would I resist? Would I rationalize that she might be wrong by using the other positive feedback to justify my performance? Would I allow my own insecurities to skew the data and hold me back? No, I wanted the truth. I wanted candid feedback. She delivered not only some very helpful ideas but a very positive lead on where I could get some training on effective presentation skills. I listened. I followed her lead. I enrolled in the workshop she suggested. I travelled to

Chicago to attend the event, despite the fact that I could barely afford it. And now I reap the benefits, a return on my investment that is beyond calculation.

How will you respond the next time
you get candid feedback?

CHECKLIST FOR SUCCESS:

☐ I take time each day to reflect on my performance.

☐ I seek the truth, even if it hurts.

☐ I look for correlations between inputs and outputs, my efforts and my results.

☐ I recognize that ego and pride can limit me from stepping up.

☐ I seek on-going improvement.

☐ I leverage my strengths and find ways to offset my limitations.

TAKE TIME

"Things which matter most must never be at the mercy of things which matter least."

~ Goethe

How often do you hear people use time as an excuse to not get something done? I hear it quite frequently. In fact, it is one of the most common excuses (inputs) that limit successful outputs. If we don't take time for what really matters, we cannot possibly expect an improvement in results. As Albert Einstein once noted, insanity is doing the same thing over and over again and expecting different results. The real key then is not the amount of time we have. We all have 24 hours in a day. It is how we prioritize our activities and use the time we have.

SUCCESS HAS MANY COMPONENTS.

We want to feel healthy.
We want to feel safe.
We want to feel financially and emotionally secure.
We want to feel loved and appreciated.
We want to feel connected to something meaningful
and important.
We want to feel we are adding value.
We want to feel like winners.

Stepping up to manifest this in one way or another requires that we identify the critical inputs to achieve these desired outputs. This translates into setting clear priorities. Wasting time on unimportant, non-critical activities—often confused as priorities—becomes the enemy, the force against us. Put another way, stepping up requires letting go.

Take time now to contemplate some of the tendencies and habits you can let go of.

Consider:

What you do with your time
What you do with your resources and money
What you do with your relationships
What you eat and drink and do with your body
What you think and believe and do with your mind
What you do with your faith

Pick one factor in each category (an input factor) and let it go. For example, consider letting go of one unhealthy substance like processed sugar, one limiting belief like "I'm not worthy," one unnecessary time-waster like meaningless gossip, television or Internet-surfing, one expensive habit, one unforgiving grudge, one emotional bag or one disempowering excuse. Let these things go. Free yourself from the emotional baggage and time-wasters in your life. Lighten your load. Discontinue or delegate the non-essential activities in your life. Give yourself space. Prepare ahead. Open your own door to opportunity. If you have staff working for you, help them do the same thing. Eliminate the non-critical activity and delegate more responsibility.

In my first management job, I learned to do exactly this. We eliminated over 50 percent of the activity in the department within six months. By removing the non-value-added time-wasters, we freed up time to take on much more important work. This benefitted the staff and it allowed me to be in a position to soon step up and accept a promotion. Some refer to this as the wisdom of emptiness. We have to empty the bowl in order to refill it. A full bowl can accept no more.

Stop and ask yourself.

What do you have in your bowl?

How effective are you at delegation and empowerment?

Are you clearing the way for higher performance
without increased stress?

Have you positioned yourself to take on more
without overflowing?

CHECKLIST FOR SUCCESS:

☐ I set goals and establish priorities every day.

☐ I identify time-wasting activity and eliminate it.

☐ I seek to simplify the complex, not complicate the simple.

☐ I let go of the things that do not matter.

☐ I manage time; time does not manage me.

☐ I do not use time as an excuse.

☐ I give myself some free time every day.

"Take care of the minutes and the hours will take care of themselves."

~ Lord Chesterfield

#5

TAKE MEASURE

"What gets measured gets improved."

~ Peter Drucker

Stepping up successfully requires credibility. People have to believe you and they have to believe in you. Sometimes you only get one chance at an opportunity. The playing field can be very competitive, so when this chance is given it is important to get it right. It is important to be prepared with good information and use the opportunity to advance your team. Results speak loudly.

What does it take to build credibility?

This is a question I am asked frequently and it is an essential part of any leadership program I offer. Credibility is absolutely fundamental to successfully leading people. Without it, shadows of doubt creep into the relationship and vital energy and confidence are lost. High-performing teams thrive on positive energy and winning expectations. People stepping up must demonstrate this winning attitude.

Credibility is gained when we are perceived as knowing what we are doing.

☐ We get the facts. We know the score.

☐ We see the big picture.

☐ We use good metrics and data to tell a compelling story.

☐ We know what we are doing and what we are talking about.

☐ We use careful analysis and good judgment to pitch alternatives and potential solutions to problems.

☐ We conduct risk analysis to avoid being perceived as careless.

☐ We turn data into information and information into knowledge.

☐ We avoid getting caught in the weeds and the minutia of the problem.

☐ We speak a language our audience can understand with context as well as content.

☐ We simplify the complex, rather than complicate the simple.

☐ We use sage leadership principles to exude patience and wisdom and avoid uninformed, opinionated debates.

☐ We value time and we demonstrate good use of it.

Taking measure means using good "intelligence" to focus, align and mobilize people. It is often what wins championships in sports, battles in war, votes in elections and new contracts in business. It means getting the facts and displaying them in an informative and inspiring way. It means knowing your audience, your players and your competition. It means building a sense of urgency by creating a clear business case that makes sense to people and inspires them to take action. Effective leaders often let the data speak for itself. A few brutal facts can be quite compelling. A good picture or graph can paint a thousand words.

I frequently use this take-away to help people around the world make stunning progress leading change quickly without any actual authority at all. For example, I teach high potential employees in organizations—often referred to as Lean Six Sigma "black belts"—to influence senior executives to make major systems changes. Ultimately, this results in culture change, a shift in organizational consciousness and behavior. These change agents require credibility to be taken seriously. How do they gain it?

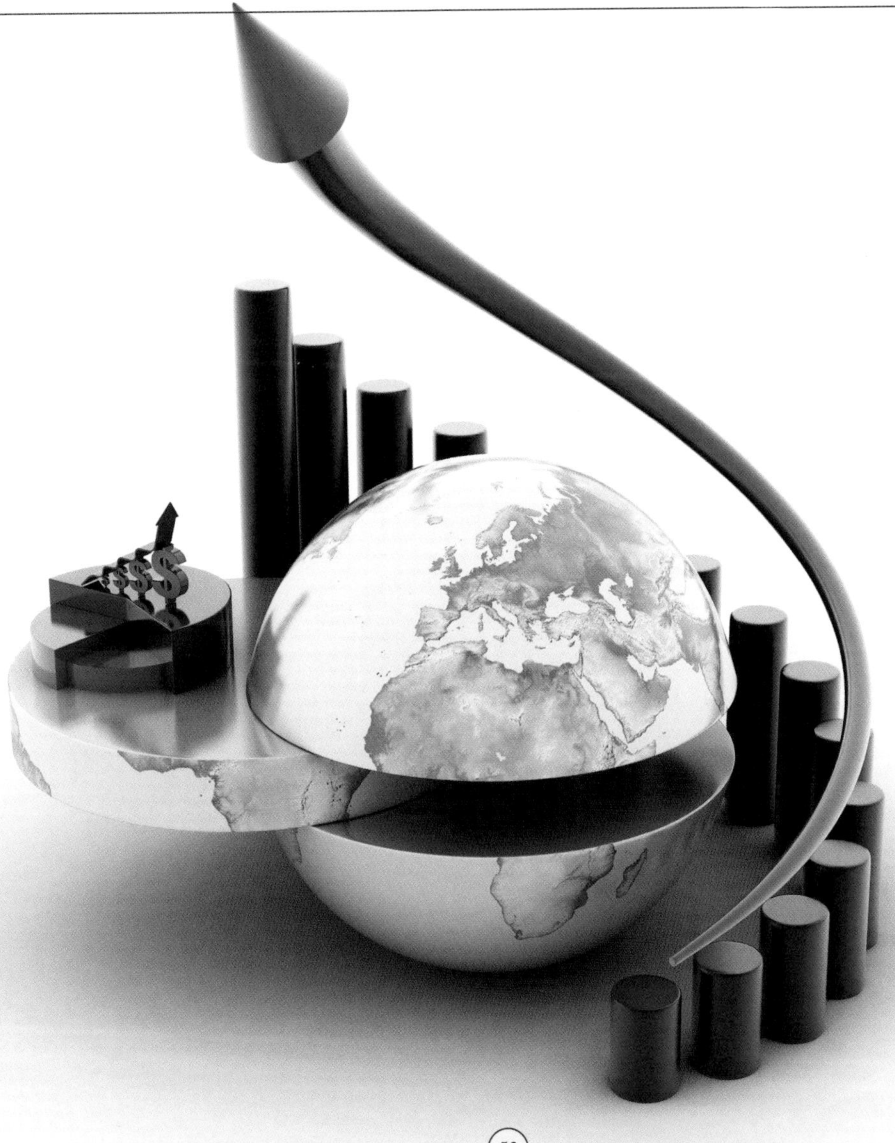

- [ ] They collect facts and data and meaningful statistics.
- [ ] They then turn the data into "a-ha" information and increased awareness.
- [ ] They educate up.
- [ ] They use rational problem-solving methods and critical thinking techniques to explore options, assess risk, calculate return on investment, and present solid business cases.
- [ ] They "wow" their bosses and their bosses' bosses—all without any formal authority at all.

As a business consultant and executive coach, I have to do the same thing. I do not have any formal positional authority in my assignments. I cannot make anyone do anything.

To inspire and lead change, I have to use influence, a subtle form of power.

Knowledge is also a form of power. Knowledge and influence can be gained when we pay attention to the facts, take measure, and turn useful data into meaningful intelligence.

Stepping up requires good intelligence.

Skill is not enough.

Use this take-away to bring something
meaningful to the table.

Use this take-away to "wow" people.

CHECKLIST FOR SUCCESS:

☐ I get the facts and check my assumptions.

☐ I do not jump to conclusions.

☐ I seek useful intelligence.

☐ I use rational methods to solve problems, mitigate risk and resolve conflict.

☐ I explain context as well as content.

☐ I pay attention to what matters and measure what I intend to manage.

#6

TAKE ADVICE

"A man's mind stretched to a new idea
never regains its original dimensions."

~ Oliver Wendell Holmes

What do all successful people have in common?
Successful people surround themselves with wise counsel and
advisors. We pay attention to who we pay attention to.

No one is successful alone. Arrogance and stubbornness obstruct
flow. Resistance to help is not helpful. A strong defense without a
strong offense is not enough to win championships. Protecting the
status quo does not foster creativity, innovation and advancement.
It grounds us in the past. It is unnatural and often quite destructive.
Change is a given. Growth is natural. Energy is meant to flow.
People resisting this sacred blessing—for whatever reasons—fall
behind. It is wise to take advice from the wise.

What kind of advice do you listen to?
Where is it coming from?
Have you ever noticed that some people are very quick
to give advice about something they know very little about?

And there are plenty of people asking for it and
listening to it—without considering the source!
Pay attention.
Examples exist everywhere.

• We have friends offering opinions and advice on subjects they
know nothing about. • We have parents directing us without
relevant training and expertise. • We have educators teaching us
practices they have not yet practiced for themselves. • We have
unhealthy marketers and advertisers telling us what to eat and
drink and do to be healthy—without any basis in fact. • We have
celebrities without subject matter expertise suggesting how we
should think and act and vote. • We have self-selected experts
and bloggers telling us how to solve problems these "experts"
have not yet solved for themselves. • We have distressed people
telling us how to reduce stress. • We have doctors and healthcare
professionals who have very limited training in nutrition and
prevention prescribing drugs with countless side effects. • We
have bosses who are in over their heads telling us how to swim.

Of course, there are many exceptions to these examples and people generally do offer advice with positive intent. Just remember, content—and not just intent—does matter.

Competence is a major factor!

When I started my consulting business in 1988, I had very little knowledge on how to build a successful practice. I had ideas. I had a vision. I had a variety of business and management experiences that would help. I had every intention of stepping up and doing it right. But I had not yet done it. I did not know what I did not know. In a word, I was ignorant. This would be a limiting factor. This would be my greatest competition. What could I do about my own ignorance?

Recognizing this gap in my plan, I set out to learn everything I could from wise and trusted experts. I listened to consultants who had been there, done that. I read books on the subject from credible and competent authorities. I surrounded myself with experienced professionals and asked for honest and candid feedback on my ideas and performance. Several of my books are actually suggestions from some of these wise and trusted allies. I also challenged much

of the advice I was offered from questionable sources. There was certainly plenty of that— including a list of things I would never be able to do effectively, like write professionally or be published! Again, two roads diverged in the mystery of life, and I choose a road less traveled.

CHECKLIST FOR SUCCESS:

☐ I surround myself with wise and trusted counsel.

☐ I embrace change.

☐ I suspend judgment and allow my mind to stretch and imagine.

☐ I pay attention to who I pay attention to – Is this source competent and reliable?

☐ I listen to and try new ideas.

☐ I take responsibility for my own ignorance.

☐ I explore multiple options before making a choice.

To accept good advice is but to increase
one's own ability."

~ Goethe

TAKE A CHANCE

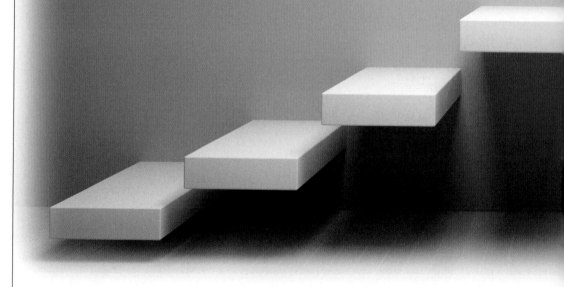

"Only those who will risk going too far
can possibly find out how far one can go."

~ T.S. Eliot

On my journey and countless attempts at stepping up, I did not always use these take-aways in the right order. For example, there have been a number of occasions where I took chances without good data and wise counsel. I now write these off as lessons learned, another term for take-aways.

In 1995, I invested in Take-Away #6: Take Advice. I will never forget sitting in a book publishing conference in Orlando, Florida. This was a conference aimed at helping authors, publishers, literary agents, editors, book marketers and distributors by providing wise and experienced counsel on the industry. As a young author with two books self-published, I figured it might offer me some very useful and profitable tricks of the trade. As part of the conference, several concurrent workshops were held allowing authors to meet with publishing experts to get feedback on their work. The feedback on my first two books was simple. I did a lot of things wrong! My book covers were not industry savvy. There were no bar codes on the cover. The books didn't "look right." I had a weak marketing and distribution plan. The list went on and on. In fact, the only thing the experts could not really explain is how the books sold out so fast. My first printing of 3,000 copies sold in less than a year. In fact, that first book, titled *Pulling Together: The*

Power of Teamwork, still sells widely on Amazon.com. It also got the attention of Mac Anderson, who now has an abbreviated version of the book on Simple Truths' top 10 best-seller list. What would the world be like without mistakes!

> Taking a chance means taking a risk.
> It translates into heart and soul and passion.
> No one is truly successful without putting their
> heart into their work. Fear is a great de-motivator.
> It inhibits us from doing things we might easily
> do—if only we weren't afraid. It is a weak management
> strategy, driven primarily by insecurity and ego.
> Fear is often a technique used by cowards, people
> limited and trapped by their own fears.

Empowerment is the removal of fear and the elimination of obstacles to success. It is what allows flow to take its energetic course. By opening the valve, the water flows. By taking a chance, life happens. By stepping up, the view gets better, even if we stumble a bit along the way. One of the great authors and consultants I followed as I was getting started in business is Tom Peters. Tom has written many best-selling books on management and leadership and I have gained a lot by listening to him. At one point in the 1980s, he told me that what people really need to do is learn to make their mistakes faster! I was intrigued by this statement because it sounded so backwards. What made it even more powerful is that he publicly made this claim during the Total Quality Management era, when most consultants were insisting that we had to get things right the first time. As I look back on my life, I hardly ever got anything right the first time. This doesn't mean I didn't try. It just means that we might never have all the facts and data we need to do a complete analysis.

Sometimes we have to act on intuition and instinct.

Sometimes decisions cannot wait.

Sometimes we just have to step up and take a chance.

The wise and successful refer to this as **courage**.

CHECKLIST FOR SUCCESS:

☐ I am willing to take a chance.

☐ I have faith in positive outcomes.

☐ I confront my fears and limiting beliefs.

☐ I see mistakes as learning opportunities.

☐ I take time to assess risk and then find ways to mitigate it.

☐ I see life as an exciting adventure full of uncertainty and opportunity.

"Why not go out on a limb?
Isn't that where the fruit is?"

~ Frank Scully

#8

TAKE ACTION

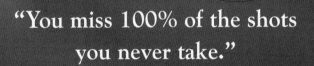

"You miss 100% of the shots
you never take."

~ Wayne Gretzky

On a recent project in Canada, I was working with a team to overhaul a production management system for a selected group of products. Included on the team were two "black belts" training in Lean Six Sigma and Operational Excellence. These belts were facilitating the project along with the project leader, the project team and me. The project was two months underway and we were on schedule, planning a launch within the next month. It was summer and one of the two "belts" scheduled a three-week vacation to visit family in Vietnam.

When he returned from Vietnam, he was surprised to see the project up and running in pilot mode. In fact, it had been running now for two weeks. Data was being collected and was showing very positive results. The 56-day cycle time was running at 16 days. Product throughput was nearly triple. Instead of using twelve assets to handle the load, we were using five. Uptime on some of these assets was two to three times the average. Millions of dollars in backorders with one of the products in this stream were eliminated. Schedule adherence on this family of products was better than anyone at this site had ever seen. The team clearly stepped up—fast!

The decision to take action so quickly in this case was encouraged and supported by the site leadership team. We were well ahead of schedule and our project team felt comfortable accepting the challenge. Clearly there was some risk, but it was time to take action and test our new design. It was time to step up as a team. Success requires action. Accelerating success requires bold action. When opportunity presents itself, we need to step up to the plate. We have to risk striking out to get a hit. One cannot exist without the other.

Action has consequence,
one way or another.
Accept it.
Embrace it.
Deal with it.
Learn from it.
ENJOY IT!

Let your job be your playing field.

Let your current situation,
whatever it is, be your platform.

Listen for that word "action" and seize it.

Build the support network you need.

Learn what you must learn
to gain confidence and credibility.

Be prepared so that when the lights
inevitably come on you can
set a positive example for others to follow.

Do not delay.

Do not procrastinate.

Do not make excuses.

People love heroes because heroes demonstrate courage. Heroes step up to the challenges and adversities they face and pave the way for others to follow. Heroes overcome the odds. Heroes live and die with honor and passion and conviction. Why not do the same? Why not unleash the giant you hold inside, the one named Spirit?

Inspiring others requires being "In Spirit." This translates into being fearless and without doubt. It means being passionate and determined to do whatever it takes to realize your dreams. With passion comes great energy and flow. Successful people use this energy to overcome odds and accomplish what many people only dream of. Look for this passion in your own heart. Channel it into your work and your relationships. Use this sacred energy to light up the world.

The opportunity is at your door. Prepare yourself and open it.

CHECKLIST FOR SUCCESS:

☐ I am proactive.

☐ I am assertive.

☐ I like being on the "playing field" and "in the game."

☐ I give my very best effort every chance I get.

☐ I do not live with regrets.

☐ I choose to live with passion.

#9

TAKE ANOTHER LOOK

"The unexamined life is not worth living."

~ Socrates

In the military, there is a term called AAR or After Action Review. Athletes, actors, speakers, and professionals use a similar process for reviewing results and making adjustments, often using video replay to carefully critique performance. My clients use AARs and video replay to gain a better understanding of process flow and to identify improvement ideas. It is remarkable to see what we see when we step up and take the time to examine it.

High-performing individuals and teams recognize that life is full of variables. Things change. New technologies are born. Paradigms shift. Innovation introduces us to new options, alternatives and best practices. We need to act, and then we need to react. Use "after action reviews" to reflect on where you are at any given time and what you might need to change to experience even better results. Use video and other feedback tools to critique your performance and solicit ideas on how to improve your game. A world of change requires frequent adjustments.

Two practices I now use daily are meditation and contemplation. Meditation allows me to ground myself in the present and reflect on the moment. Often we are so caught up in the past or the future, we miss the only time that really matters—the now! By taking time each morning and throughout the day to step back, breathe deeply, let go of tension and stress, find my center, evaluate my priorities and proceed with a sense of calm and composure, I feel better. I feel more confident. I feel more secure. I feel more at ease.

The same is true for contemplation. This practice simply means that I consider various points of view without criticism and judgment. I simply listen and seek understanding. When our minds are already made up about something, we limit our growth.

How can we be so sure we are right?

Very seldom does anyone have all the facts.
Very seldom does anyone know the absolute truth.

How arrogant is it to assume we do?

Confusing assumptions with facts leads to more conflict and stress than anything else.
It gives birth to war, divorce, hostility and hatred.

Why not open our minds to new insights and possibilities?

Taking another look can apply to anything. We can use this take-away to re-evaluate our relationships, our jobs, our performance, our limitations, our perceptions, our assumptions, our judgments, our successes and our failures.

What is working for us and what is not?

What is allowing us to grow and prosper and what is holding us back?

What excuses do we hear ourselves using and what alternatives exist?

What beliefs do we hold to be true that just might not be?

What habits are working for us and against us?

What do we tend to do and what do we tend not to do?

How is this working for us?

When I decided to start a consulting practice in 1988, I had two very capable and credible people interested in joining me. As a result, I wrote the business plan to include the unique competencies and skills these two gentlemen would bring to the table. This would give our clientele a more comprehensive menu of services and a deeper level of experience. Less than six months into our first year, both of my colleagues decided that the entrepreneurial venture was not for them. The risk was just too great. They needed to cut the cord. Clearly this was a set-back, but as the future would reveal, it was not the end of the company. I stepped back, rewrote the business plan, redefined the services I would offer, made several necessary adjustments and stepped back into the game. I took the road less traveled.

No regrets.

If you have not already done so, make this take-away a daily habit. It is during our moments of reflection and release that ingenious thoughts and ideas come our way. It is when we "let go" that we "let flow." Take a moment now to contemplate one or two things you can do immediately to step up and shine. Is there a project at work you can volunteer to help with? Is there a need at home you can take on without complaint? Is there a gap in your relationship with someone that you can close by apologizing or taking ownership? Is there a time-waster in your daily routine you can unload? Is there someone you can help? You know the answer is yes. There is no shortage of opportunity to make adjustments and step up.

The only thing really holding people back is that inner voice that says "can't."

Use the word "can" and you are already one step ahead.

CHECKLIST FOR SUCCESS:

☐ I use AARs daily to reflect on and critique my performance.

☐ I realize that high performance requires making adjustments along the way.

☐ I understand that there is more than one way to do things.

☐ I challenge the status quo.

☐ I pioneer change.

☐ I believe in continuous improvement.

TAKE A KNEE

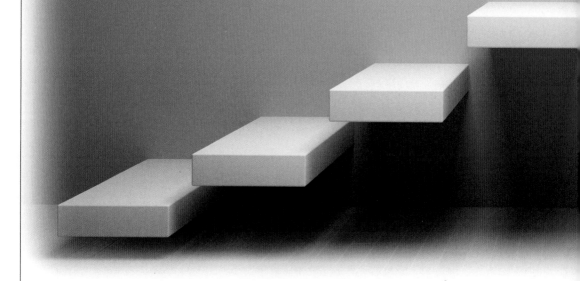

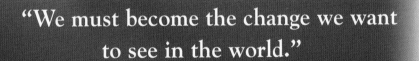

"We must become the change we want
to see in the world."

~ Gandhi

Take a knee can mean many things. This is intentional so I leave the interpretation up to you.

When I was playing football, take a knee meant we need to talk. We need to go over something important or review what is going on. Take a knee meant pay attention! When I am in church, take a knee means show respect, offer prayer and give thanks. It is considered an act of humility, service, praise and gratitude. In some circles, take a knee means being crowned, knighted or honored in some way—a form of recognition for stepping up. To many people, take a knee symbolizes proposing for marriage, making a promise or offering a lifelong commitment. It can also mean taking a bow. Be gracious. Be humble. Accept the support and applause you are getting. Acknowledge and honor it.

Truly successful people give credit where credit is due. We look for ways to make other people look good. We look for ways to help other people step up and manifest success. We view life as "cooperation," not a competition. We wake up each day looking for win-win propositions, not ego-driven, win-lose strategies based on the scarcity assumption. At the end of the day, we feel good about the opportunity we have, the lives we touch and the bounties we receive. Metaphorically and often literally, we take a knee to focus attention, give thanks and praise, renew our promises and accept the abundance we have.

Gratitude is a powerful form of energy. It is one of the surest and fastest ways to transcend ego thinking and scarcity consciousness. By giving thanks for what we have, rather than dwelling on feelings of lack or disappointment, we call forth into our lives more abundance, more success and more joy. We manifest what we dwell on, so if we feel grateful for what we have, we attract more positive results into our lives. If we dwell on lack or the absence of something, we experience lack. If we dwell on stress, we feel stressed. The universe delivers what we deliver. The cosmic mirror does not lie.

I have had many hardships and setbacks
in my life. Some of these I share in this book
to make a point.

THE POINT IS THIS:
we all have crosses to bear.
We all have adversity to overcome.

These are the great lessons in life. These are the perfect opportunities to step up. Without these challenges, we cannot know who we are and what we are really capable of. Without contrast, there can be no understanding. What is light without darkness? What is up without down?

Take a knee often and appreciate what you have—physically, mentally, emotionally and spiritually.

Make it a daily habit.

Take a knee and see the opportunity you are given.

Take a knee and welcome the help you have surrounding you.

Take a knee and feel good.

Life is a journey, one step at a time.

Pay attention to the now.

Be present.

Be yourself.

Fear not and enjoy the adventure.

CHECKLIST FOR SUCCESS:

- ☐ I appreciate what I have.

- ☐ I give thanks daily.

- ☐ I let go of past "baggage" and grief.

- ☐ I let go of worry and guilt.

- ☐ I give credit where credit is due.

- ☐ I recognize that I am part of something much greater than myself.

STEP UP
OR
STEP ASIDE

"The ladder of success is best climbed
by stepping on the rungs
of opportunity."

~ Ayn Rand

Not everyone wants to step up. That makes it easier for those who do. There is less traffic on the leading edge. Some people would rather wait and see. Others prefer the bleachers, watching the action from a "safe" distance. They have no intention of getting in the game and there is nothing wrong with this. It gives us contrast. Ultimately, stepping up is a matter of personal choice. Two roads diverge in life and we are given the opportunity to choose.

This book is not written for the timid or hesitant. It is not aimed at the armchair quarterback or skeptical critic. It is not intended for the professional excuse-maker or resistant ego dweller. These folks can step aside. Indeed, they already have. This book is written for the rising stars, legacies in the making. This is a book for heroes in disguise, names we may recognize one day for truly making a difference. It is for agents of change, not victims of change.

Organizational leaders worldwide are calling for people to step up. Governments value it. Corporations value it. School systems value it. Hospitals value it. Successful people value it. What we don't value are excuses. We don't value resistance to positive change. We don't value rationalizations for the problems we face. Common beliefs—like I am too old, or I am too young, or I am the wrong race or gender or nationality or creed—do not help you step up. They matter only if you make them matter. They limit you only if you allow them to limit you by dwelling on them in a negative, disempowering way. Stepping up is about stepping over excuses and resistance. It is about transcending fear and blame and limiting beliefs. It is about pointing your finger at the target, not at your teammate.

Use the take-aways and checklists in this book to guide you on your journey. These are proven "lessons learned" that apply globally and universally. Look for them in happy, healthy, successful people around you. Pay attention to them. Practice them at your own pace. Make the adjustments you will undoubtedly have to make. Recognize that success is a journey and not a bench along the way or a future destination. It is here and now, every step of the way. It is a state of mind and a state of being. It is the feeling you have when you are truly happy and sincerely thankful. Use these take-aways to sharpen your focus, lighten your load and step up without fear.

The climb is healthy and the view is terrific!

JOHN J. MURPHY

John J. Murphy is an award-winning author, speaker and management consultant. Drawing on a diverse collection of team experiences as a corporate manager, consultant and collegiate quarterback, John has appeared on over 400 radio and television stations and his work has been featured in over 50 newspapers nationwide.

As founder and president of Venture Management Consultants, www.venturemanagementconsultants.com, John specializes in creating high performance team environments, teaching leadership and team development, and leading global kaizen events. He has trained thousands of "change agents" from over 50 countries and helped some of the world's leading organizations design and implement positive change.

John is a critically-acclaimed author and sought-after speaker. Among his other books are: *Pulling Together: 10 Rules for High Performance Teams, Beyond Doubt: Four Steps to Inner Peace, Sage Leadership: Awakening the Spirit in Work, Reinvent Yourself: A Lesson in Personal Leadership, Agent of Change: Leading a Cultural Revolution, Get a Real Life: A Lesson in Personal Empowerment, The Eight Disciplines: An Enticing Look Into Your Personality, Habits Die Hard: 10 Steps to Building Successful Habits, Leading with Passion: 10 Essentials for Inspiring Others,* and *The How of Wow: Secrets to World Class Service.*

WHAT OTHERS ARE SAYING...

We purchased a Simple Truths' gift book for our conference in Lisbon, Spain. We also personalized it with a note on the first page about valuing innovation. I've never had such positive feedback on any gift we've given. People just keep talking about how much they valued the book and how perfectly it tied back to our conference message.

— Michael R. Marcey, Efficient Capital Management, LLC.

The small inspirational books by Simple Truths are amazing magic! They spark my spirit and energize my soul.

— Jeff Hughes, United Airlines

Mr. Anderson, ever since a friend of mine sent me the 212° movie online, I have become a raving fan of Simple Truths. I love and appreciate the positive messages your products convey and I have found many ways to use them. Thank you for your vision.

— Patrick Shaughnessy, AVI Communications, Inc.

If you have enjoyed this book we invite you to check out our entire collection of gift books, with free inspirational movies, at www.simpletruths.com. You'll discover it's a great way to inspire friends and family, or to thank your best customers and employees.

The
simple truths®
Difference

For more information, please visit us at:

www.simpletruths.com

Or call us toll free... 800-900-3427